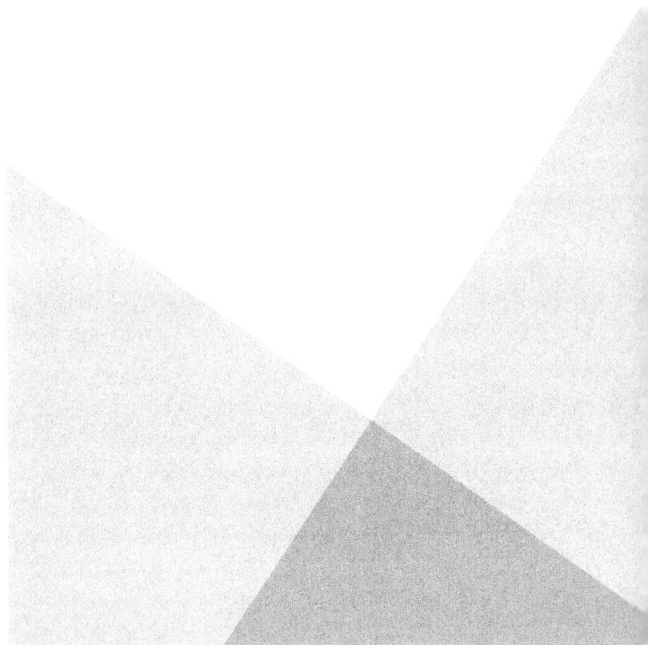

BOOK ANALYSIS

By Verity Roat

The Goldfinch

BY DONNA TARTT

Bright
≡Summaries.com

DONNA TARTT

AMERICAN NOVELIST AND SHORT STORY WRITER

- **Born in Greenwood, Mississippi (USA) in 1963.**
- **Notable works:**
  - *The Secret History* (1992), novel
  - *The Little Friend* (2002), novel

Donna Tartt was born in Greenwood, Mississippi and grew up in nearby Grenada. Her father was a successful local politician, Don Tartt. At 13, Tartt was published for the first time when she submitted a sonnet to a Mississippi literary review. She enrolled in the University of Mississippi in 1981, where she caught the attention of Willie Morris (American writer and editor, 1934-1999). Morris admitted Tartt onto his graduate writing programme when she was only an 18-year-old freshman. Tartt's work is written largely in a neo-romantic style influenced heavily by 19th-century literature. She has published three novels, as well as a handful of short stories.

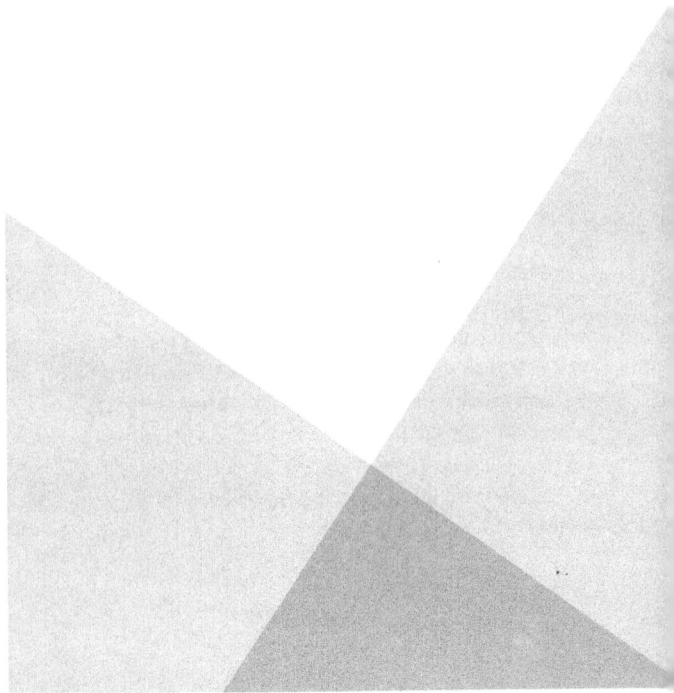

THE GOLDFINCH

A COMING-OF-AGE NARRATIVE OF A TEENAGE BOY'S DESCENT INTO THE WORLD OF CRIME

- **Genre:** novel
- **Reference edition:** Tartt, D. (2013) *The Goldfinch*. London: Little, Brown.
- **1st edition:** 2013
- **Themes:** art and aesthetics, alcohol and drug abuse, friendship, morality and crime, love and relationships, death and grief, trauma

The Goldfinch is narrated in the first person by its protagonist, Theo Decker, who retrospectively tells the story of his descent into the criminal world. At the age of 13, Theo visits a museum in New York with his mother, who is keen to see an exhibition which includes one of her favourite paintings, *The Goldfinch*, by Carel Fabritius (Dutch painter, 1622-1654). While they are there, terrorists plant a bomb which explodes, killing many of the museum's visitors, including Theo's mum. In his confusion after the explosion, Theo leaves the museum, taking *The Goldfinch* with him. The rest of the novel explores his guilt over having stolen the painting and his fear that his theft will be discovered. It also examines the effect this early trauma has on Theo's life. The novel was generally well received in both the US. and Europe, though some critics felt that its style was too Dickensian and that many of the characters were clichéd.

SUMMARY

THE EXPLOSION

When the novel begins, Theodore Decker has just been suspended from school and he and his mother are due to attend a meeting at the school with his headmaster. Before the meeting, his mother decides that they should visit an exhibition at the Metropolitan Museum of Art, which contains one of her favourite paintings, *The Goldfinch*, by Carel Fabritius. Theo is happy for any distraction from the meeting and agrees. At the museum, Theo spots an elderly gentleman and a red-headed girl who is about his age carrying a musical instrument in a case. He is fascinated by this girl and quickly becomes infatuated with her. When his mother decides to go into another room in the exhibition, Theo hangs back to look at *The Goldfinch*. Unfortunately, a bomb, which has been planted by terrorists, explodes, killing Theo's mother, as well as several other patrons of the museum.

When Theo regains consciousness after the explosion, he sees the elderly man, later identified as Welton "Welty" Blackwell, lying in the rubble. Welty is slowly dying and beckons Theo over. In his deluded state, he thinks he recognises Theo and talks to him about the past, before giving him an enigmatic message asking Theo to take his ring back to his business partner, James "Hobie" Hobart. In his confusion, Theo believes that Welty is also asking him to take *The Goldfinch*, so he picks it up and leaves the museum. He then returns to his flat, expecting his mother to return.

A NEW LIFE

Shortly after the explosion, two social workers appear at the flat and tell Theo that his mother has died. Unable to find his father, they decide to send him to stay with the family of his childhood friend, Andy Barbour. Theo is quickly swept up in the very different lifestyle the wealthy Barbours lead. During his long stay with the Barbours, Theo finds Welty's address and returns the ring to Hobie. The two strike up a friendship, but Theo decides to keep the painting hidden, unsure what to do with it.

Just before the Barbours and Theo are due to spend the summer on their family boat, Theo's deadbeat dad turns up at the Barbours' with his girlfriend, Xandra. He sells all of Theo's mother's possessions and takes Theo back with him to Las Vegas. Theo sneaks *The Goldfinch* onto the plane with him.

HEDONISM IN LAS VEGAS

In Las Vegas, Theo meets Boris, the young son of a Russian immigrant. The two bond over their absentee fathers and quickly become firm friends, sharing everything they have: money, drugs, alcohol and cigarettes. Theo still has not decided what to do with the painting; he wants to return it but fears he will be branded a criminal, so he keeps it wrapped in layers of duct tape and newspaper in a pillow case stuck to the back of the headboard of his bed. He has a tumultuous relationship with his father, who is an alcoholic; sometimes his father is very abusive and neglectful, leaving Theo to find his own food and get himself to school, and sometimes he can be very generous and kind, giving Theo large sums of money and taking him, Xandra and Boris out for dinner. He also has money troubles, and occasionally gangsters appear at the house and threaten Theo.

One night, Xandra returns home from work and tells Theo that his father has died in a drunk driving accident. Afraid of being sent to live with his grandparents or falling into the care system, Theo runs away back to New York.

IN NEW YORK AGAIN

When Theo returns to New York, he does not know who else to seek out, so he goes to Hobie's shop, where he meets the red-headed girl, Pippa, again. Hobie agrees with Theo's lawyer to let Theo stay with him. Theo manages to get his life somewhat back on track: he stops smoking, drinking and taking illegal drugs (though he remains reliant on prescription painkillers), and finishes his schooling and goes on to university, where he scrapes by. Pippa, who is dealing with long-term illness after the explosion, is sent to live with her aunt to convalesce. After university, Theo joins Hobie's business selling antiques. Aware that the business is in a lot of debt, Theo takes some of the articles Hobie has made as a hobby and sells them as genuine antiques. He also reconnects with the Barbours; sadly Andy and his father were killed in a boating accident, but he becomes close with Mrs Barbour and ends up engaged to Kitsey Barbour, Andy's younger sister. Theo's fortunes change when a disgruntled customer realises he has been sold a fake. He attempts to blackmail Theo, saying he knows the whereabouts of *The Goldfinch*. Around the same time, Boris comes back into Theo's life and confesses that he stole the painting when they were in high school. He has since used it as collateral in his illegal business dealing and as a consequence has lost the painting.

RETRIEVING THE PAINTING

On the night of Theo's engagement party, Boris turns up and says he has located the painting. He flies the two of them to Amsterdam, where they steal the painting back. However, the gangsters who stole the painting realise what has happened and send men to kill Boris and Theo. Theo shoots and kills one of them, but not before the gangsters manage to take the painting again. Boris learns the whereabouts of the painting and decides to have one of his business partners anonymously inform the police. He shares the reward money with Theo.

At the end of the novel, Theo has returned to New York and wonders if the events of the novel were due to fate or some irreparable character trait of his.

CHARACTER STUDY

THEO DECKER

Theo is the protagonist of *The Goldfinch* and retrospectively narrates the story. He is 13 years old at the beginning of the novel, when he is present during an explosion in the Metropolitan Museum of Art in New York, which kills his mother. In the confusion after the explosion, he takes *The Goldfinch* from the museum. Throughout the rest of the novel, he struggles with guilt over his mother's death and over the theft of the painting. Abused and neglected by his alcoholic father, he relies on alcohol, drugs and cigarettes, and eventually becomes involved in the criminal underworld. He also spends the majority of the novel infatuated with Pippa, the red-headed girl he spots in the museum. The two become very close, but never become romantically involved, as Pippa believes their shared trauma would place too much of a strain on their relationship. In many respects, Theo is the archetypal central character of a *Bildungsroman* (coming-of-age novel), as he is a young man whose story progresses from his youth to young adulthood.

AUDREY DECKER

Theo's mother dies in the explosion at the beginning of the novel. Theo describes her as very beautiful and creative, though her education and career were limited due to her abusive relationship with Theo's father. He is very close to her up to her death, which then haunts him as he feels responsible for it.

LARRY DECKER

Larry is Theo's alcoholic father. He disappeared from Theo's life a year before the explosion happened. Before he left, his presence in Theo's life was very tumultuous, swinging between elation during his drunk periods and anger and melancholy every time he tried to quit drinking. He reappears several months after Audrey's death and takes Theo to Las Vegas, where he continues to behave in the same way he had done before he left. He even attempts to gain access to the money left to Theo by his mother in order to pay off his gambling debts. His self-destructive behaviours and self-inflicted death (he was drunk driving and crashed) cause Theo to examine his own behaviour and self-destructive tendencies.

BORIS PAVLIKOVSKY

Boris is Theo's best friend in Las Vegas:

> "He was pale and thin, not very clean, with lank dark hair falling in his eyes and the unwholesome wanness of a runaway, callused hands and black-circled nails chewed to the nub" (p. 263)

He and Theo bond over their shared experience of abusive, alcoholic fathers, and he introduces Theo to darker indulgences, such as alcohol and illegal drugs. On one drunken evening, Theo shows Boris *The Goldfinch*, which Boris later decides to steal. He turns up again later in Theo's life and eventually retrieves the painting, returns it to the museum and splits the reward money with Theo. Despite his lack of education and difficult upbringing, Boris is intelligent and crafty: he speaks several languages fluently and is a successful (if somewhat illicit) businessman.

JAMES "HOBIE" HOBART

When Theo meets Welty after the explosion in the museum, he asks Theo to take his ring to his business partner, Hobie. The two ran an antiques business together. Hobie is delighted to receive the ring and becomes friends with Theo. When Theo returns to New York from Las Vegas, Hobie takes him in and the two eventually work together in the antiques business. He finally provides Theo with a little stability in his life and is very forgiving of all of Theo's transgressions.

PIPPA

Pippa is the red-headed girl that Theo spots in the museum. He is instantly attracted to her and is delighted when she reappears in his life when he turns up at Hobie's. She suffers from complications due to a head injury which she sustained during the explosion in the museum. Once a talented musician, she has to give up any hopes of playing music professionally. She moves to England and finds a boyfriend, though she and Theo remain close and she does reveal that she loves him, but she feels their shared trauma would make a romantic relationship impossible for them.

ANALYSIS

MORALITY

As art theft is at the heart of the novel, it is natural that morality is one of the key themes in *The Goldfinch*. Theo impulsively takes *The Goldfinch* from the Metropolitan Museum of Art after a bomb planted by terrorists explodes there. For the rest of the novel, he is wracked with guilt, both over his mother's death and over the theft of the painting. For a long time, he is unsure what to do with the painting; as a young teenager, he wishes to return it to the museum, but is scared of the consequences. During his stay at the Barbours', Theo thinks: "At some point I was going to have to get it back to the museum, though I still hadn't quite figured out how I was going to do that without causing a huge fuss" (p. 113). So it is clear that he knows what, morally, he should do, but feels helpless and unable to actually do it. Later on, he feels sentimentally attached to the painting because his mother adored it, and is therefore loath to give it up. He says: "It wasn't that I minded giving it back; if I could have returned it magically, by wishing, I would have done it in a second. It was just that I couldn't think how to return it in a way that wouldn't endanger either me or the painting" (p. 195). When Theo and Boris are in Amsterdam retrieving the painting, Boris exhibits a different perception of morality; he tricks the people who have the painting into believing he will pay the ransom and then does not at the last minute:

> "Because we lucked out! [...] Once in a lifetime chance! We had the opportunity! What were they going to do? They were two – we were four. If they had any sense, they should never have let us inside. And – yes, I know, only forty thousand, but why should I pay them one cent if I don't have to? For stealing my own property?" (p. 750)

Theo is horrified by this as it potentially jeopardises the painting and because Boris pulls out a gun, having said that he does not believe in using violence. When they finally find the painting and return it to the police for the reward money, Theo initially does not want to take his share, as he does not believe he deserves it. Right from when Theo first steals the painting, it causes him to question his morality.

Grief

Grief and society's treatment of it play a significant role in *The Goldfinch*. Many of the novel's characters experience trauma, death and grief: Theo experiences both trauma and grief when he is present during the explosion which kills his mother and because of his father's abusive nature and eventual death; Pippa experiences the same, as the explosion kills her uncle and guardian, Welty, and gives her a long-term brain injury; Hobie is aggrieved because he has lost his business partner and friend; the Barbours grieve when Andy and Mr Barbour die. Each of these characters experiences grief in an incredibly individual way, suggesting that grief is a very personal journey. If we look in particular at Theo's grief, we can see that the various adults in his life all have different expectations of how he will grieve. To begin with, he finds his mother's death incredibly painful and cannot bear to see anything which reminds him of her:

> "Steeling myself against her reading glasses on the bureau and her black tights stiff where she'd draped them to dry and her handwriting on her

> desk calendar and a million other heart-piercing sights, I picked it up and tucked it under my arm and walked quickly into my own room across the hall" (p. 210)

To protect himself, he relies on cutting himself off from other people, and as such, he barely shows any outward emotion, especially to the adults in his life. This concerns them greatly as they all have ideas about how grief should manifest itself. Slowly his grief dissipates and he begins to be able to feel happiness again, but this concerns other people, because he never appeared to actually grieve for his mother. The only person he feels comfortable with is Hobie:

> "I liked him because he treated me as a companion and conversationalist in my own right. It didn't matter that sometimes he wanted to talk about his neighbour who had a knee replacement or a concert of early music he'd seen uptown. If I told him something funny that happened at school, he was an attentive and appreciative audience; unlike Mrs. Swanson (who froze and looked startled when I made a joke) or Dave (who chuckled, but awkwardly, and always a beat too late), he liked to laugh, and I loved it when he told me stories of his own life" (p. 189)

Nonetheless, Theo is still plagued by guilt and grief, which continually cause him to question his actions on the day of the explosion:

> "If only I could go back and change what happened, keep it from happening somehow. Why hadn't I insisted we get breakfast instead of going to the museum? Why hadn't Mr. Beeman asked us to come in on Tuesday, or Thursday?" (p. 97)

In this way, Tartt explores the way that grief can be tied up with different emotions. While Theo does not display the hurt and anguish that the adults in his life think he should, he is clearly processing his grief through his guilt.

Anxiety

Theo's grief also appears to cause him a great deal of anxiety around death. Although he is often suicidal and actually attempts suicide on numerous occasions, he seems to be very afraid of death:

> "But depression wasn't the word. This was a plunge encompassing sorrow and revulsion far beyond the personal: a sick, drenching nausea

at all humanity and human endeavour from the dawn of time. The writhing loathsomeness of the biological order. Old age, sickness, death. No escape for anyone. Even the beautiful ones were like soft fruit about to spoil. And yet somehow people still kept fucking and breeding and po-pping out new fodder for the grave, producing more and more new beings to suffer like this was some kind of redemptive, or good, or even somehow morally admirable thing" (p. 534)

Through this portrayal of grief, Tartt could be suggesting that there is a link between death an-xiety and childhood trauma. As Theo experiences the death of both of his parents at such a young age, it would seem natural that his grief may lead him to become very anxious and depressed.

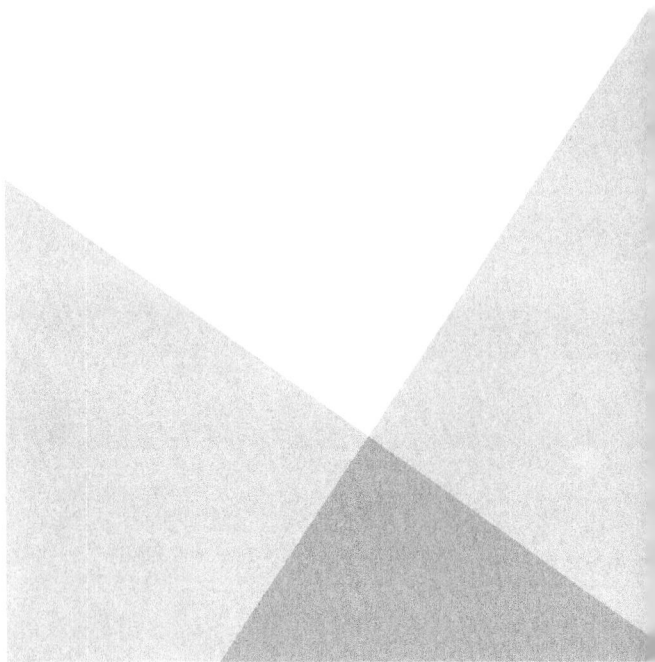

FURTHER REFLECTION

SOME QUESTIONS TO THINK ABOUT...

- When Theo goes to live with his father and Xandra, he says: "living with them was like living with roommates I didn't particularly get along with" (p. 258). Why do you think Tartt chose to describe the father-son relationship between Theo and Larry in this way?
- The theme of morality appears throughout the novel – do you think that overall Theo is a moral character? Explain with reference to his reaction to stealing *The Goldfinch*.
- How do you think Theo's life might have turned out differently if his father had not taken him away from the Barbours? In what way does this event affect the narrative of *The Goldfinch*?
- Why do you think Donna Tartt chose *The Goldfinch* (the painting by Carel Fabritius) as the painting which Theo stole from the museum? In what way could the subject matter of the painting be symbolic of events within the novel?

- What do you think motivates Theo to steal *The Goldfinch* from the museum? Why doesn't he return it earlier?
- Towards the end of the novel, Pippa tells Theo that she loves him, but does not think they are suited to a romantic relationship. Do you think that it is true that their shared trauma would put a strain on romance?
- What do you think motivates Boris to take the painting from Theo?
- Do you agree with the critics who felt that the characters in *The Goldfinch* are clichéd? Explain your answer.

We want to hear from you!
Leave a comment on your online library
and share your favourite books on social media!

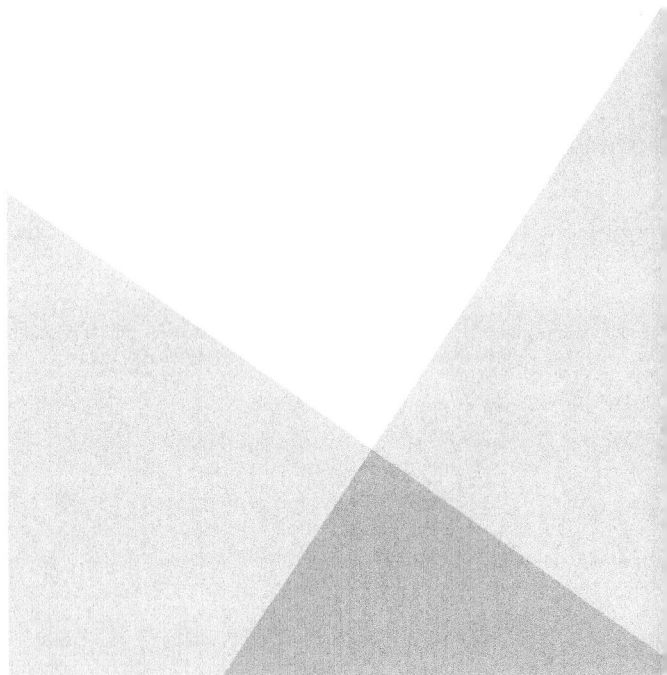

FURTHER READING

REFERENCE EDITION

- Tartt, D. (2013) *The Goldfinch*. London: Little, Brown.

ADAPTATIONS

- *The Goldfinch*. (2019) [Film]. John Crowley. Dir. USA: Warner Bros. Pictures.

MORE FROM BRIGHTSUMMARIES.COM

- Reading guide – *The Secret History* by Donna Tartt.

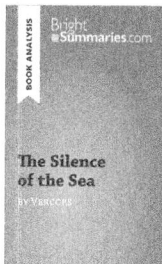

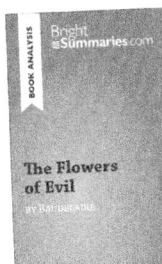

www.brightsummaries.com

Ebook EAN: 9782808019309

Paperback EAN: 9782808019316

Legal Deposit: D/2019/12603/132

Cover: © Primento

Digital conception by Primento, the digital partner of
publishers.

Printed in Great Britain
by Amazon